TAKE AWAY THE LABEL!

(AND SEE WHAT I CAN DO)

Published in 2024

Copyright 2024 Susan Hanley

Authors: Susan Hanley, Karen Murray, Jacqueline Ward, Amanda Haigh, Maggie Graham, Kath Lindley, Jan Wells, Ed Balls, Hilary Benn.

Photography: Jan Wells

All rights reserved. No part of this publication may be produced, distributed, or transmitted in any form or by any means, including photocopying, recording, or other electronic or mechanical methods, without prior written permission of the copyright holder, except in accordance with the provisions of the copyright law. Applications for the copyright holders written permission to reproduce any part of this publication should be addressed to the copyright holder.

Disclaimer: **Take Away the Label** is intended for information and education purposes only. This book does not constitute specific advice to your situation. The views and opinions expressed in this book are those of the author and do not reflect those of the editor or copyright holder. All people mentioned in the chapters have been used with permission. To the best of my knowledge the author has complied with fair usage. Future editions can be rectified if omissions are brought to authors attention.

Susan is an inspiration and living proof of the great potential within all of us. She has achieved so much because she cares and never gives up.

- Hilary Benn MP

Susan, this is Ed Balls. I just wanted to send you huge, best wishes and congratulations and thanks because you've just made such a massive difference.

We've not seen each other for a few years now. I so loved working with you and what you were doing around the 'Hear my Voice' campaign was so important and whether that was coming to the department with me or coming to my constituency or coming to our Garden party. We are still doing the same garden party every year with a brass band and a barbecue.

There's nothing that we would love more than to see you come along.

I just wanted to say you were an inspiration to me and you showed me what can be done.

You showed me what passion and commitment is all about and what I learned from that, and I've taken it with me, and I've often thought of those times with you.

So, I just wanted to say a big thank you to you and say, Susan, you are a very, very special person.

- **ED BALLS**

Former UK Shadow Chancellor of the Exchequer & Senior Fellow, Harvard Kennedy School

Ed Balls is a British Labour Party and Co-operative Party politician. He was the Member of Parliament (MP) for Normanton from 2005 to 2010 and for Morley and Outwood from 2010 to 2015.

Susan's Dedication

I have to start by thanking my family who have always been there for me, supporting me through different stages of my life and ensuring that I have stayed safe and inclusive.

I am especially grateful to my sister Jacqui and my brother-in-law Michael for giving me a loving home, and who have supported me, believed in me, and cared for me for over 40 years, without their help I would not have been able to achieve what I have.

To my other sister, Josephine who has also supported me over the years, and steps in to look after me when necessary.

Special thanks go to Mandy Haigh and Jan Wells who have supported me for several years on different projects and was there for me through a very difficult time. They have never stopped believing in me and are continuing to do so. It was Mandy and Jan who encouraged me to write about my life and what I have achieved, so, I will be forever grateful to you both for your support and the opportunities you have given me to enrich my life.

Massive, massive thanks go to my totally brilliant writer/editor Karen Murray who has patiently had weekly online meetings with me to learn about my life and what I have achieved. Karen has spent many hours researching and has been hugely supportive, patient and constantly encouraging me to talk about the various stages of my life. So thank you again Karen I am really going to miss our weekly meetings.

I also owe my thanks to so many people who have helped me on my life's journey and patiently put up with my questions and generously given me so much of their time, without which, I would have ended up invisible and just another statistic. So, a huge thank you to all those of you who I have had the pleasure of working with over the years and who have contributed to my book and my life.

A special mention goes to Kath Lindley, Maggie Graham, Janet Wright, Adam Ogilvy, Ed Balls and Hilary Benn. I really hope I have made a difference to the lives of people and especially people with a Learning Disability.

Acknowledgement

Thank you for everyone's input into my book and supporting me to piece together my incredible journey so far.

I hope you all enjoy reading.

Contents

Susan's Dedication 5

Acknowledgement 7

Chapter One: My Early Life 11

Chapter Two: Moving into Adulthood 15

Chapter Three: Self-Advocacy 21

Chapter Four: Speaking Out! 27

Chapter Five: Leep1 31

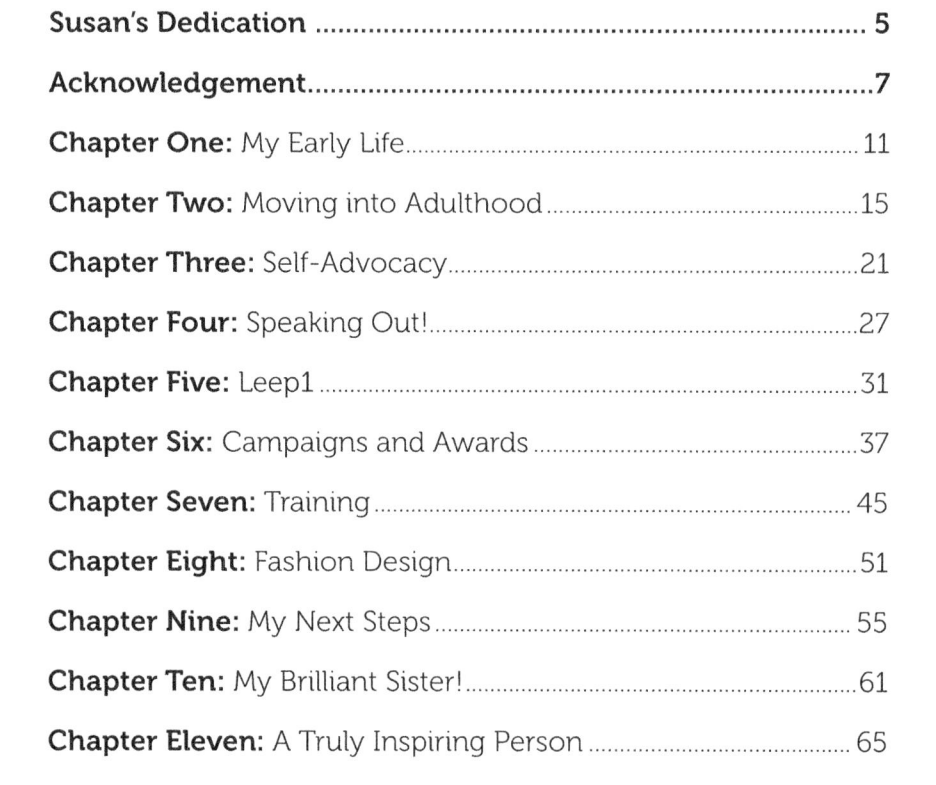

Chapter Six: Campaigns and Awards 37

Chapter Seven: Training 45

Chapter Eight: Fashion Design 51

Chapter Nine: My Next Steps 55

Chapter Ten: My Brilliant Sister! 61

Chapter Eleven: A Truly Inspiring Person 65

Chapter Twelve: Susan Hanley is a Legend! 69

Chapter Thirteen: A Brilliant Leader and Friend 73

Chapter Fourteen: Telling Susan's story 79

Chapter Fifteen 81

Chapter One:
My Early Life

When I was born in 1964 a lot of parents believed that if their child was born with Down Syndrome, they would never walk or talk or do any of the things other children could do. I have proved these people wrong.

There are about 1.5 million people in the United Kingdom with a learning disability, but they are not often recognised in society. I want to change that. People often give me funny looks and treat me differently because I have a learning disability, but they don't know me and what I can do. For a long time, I've wanted to tell people what I've done with my life and maybe someone will think, "I want to do that!"

Even though I was born with a learning disability, that doesn't mean I shouldn't have the same chances in life as everyone else. In the past I've had some bad experiences and I don't want anyone else to go through that. I want to encourage other people to speak up and make a difference to the lives of other people with a learning disability. That's what I think being a campaigner is all about and that's why I am proud to be an ambassador for people with learning disabilities in Leeds and the co-chair of Leep1.

People often tell me I'm an inspirational woman and a role model to other people and this makes me feel so proud and happy. Over the last few years, I've been lucky enough to meet and interview politicians and I think that working alongside them to help them understand what is important to people with a learning disability, is one of the best ways to make changes happen.

All I want, is to live a healthy and happy life and carry on doing the things I like doing. I am doing just that right now by sharing my life story and I plan to keep on fighting for the rights of people with a learning disability. Life is too short, and we all should do the things we want to do while we can.

So, back to the beginning. I was born in Morley near Leeds, my mum's name was Elizabeth Mary Hanley and my dad's name was Harold Hanley. They already had two older girls and a boy when I was born, so I was the baby of the family. The first home I can remember living in was a bungalow where I lived with our parents as my brother and sisters had already moved away by the time I went to school. Our home had a lovely kitchen, a bathroom and two bedrooms and outside there was a garage right next to a big wall. The wall might not have been that big it's just that I remember it as being big because I was so small.

Further down the street, I had a friend called Michelle who also had a learning disability and we used to spend hours doing colouring together with felt pens and coloured pencils. These days were special to me, and it was about this time I had a dog called Becky who was a golden retriever and later I had a rabbit with big ruby eyes who I called bright eyes. I often used to play card games with my mum, like sevens, snap and fish and each year we went to Butlin's in Skegness together where we played bingo. We usually stayed in a chalet, and I really enjoyed spending time with my mum there as it was just the two of us because my dad didn't like bingo so he stayed at home.

Mum and my auntie used to do a lot of craft work together and I enjoyed watching them making things, so my mum taught me how to knit and aunty taught me how to crochet and do needlework. This is where my love of knitting and needlework comes from and now I am very good at needlework, for example, counting, cross-stich and tapestries. Whenever I do needlework, it reminds me of the times I spent with my mum, aunty and my cousins and this makes me feel calm. That's why I love needlework so much and my passion for this has turned into designing clothing. Not very long ago, I was invited to showcase my needlework at Leeds city museum, as part of the "New Enterprise in the Community" exhibition. I felt so proud to think of my needlework, cross-stitch and tapestries being seen by so many people when they walked round the museum and it was lovely to talk to people about my work on opening night.

My dad Harold loved to play golf and was president of the Fulneck Golf Club near Pudsey for a couple of years, and I often went there with him. Sometimes, he did the catering there or took his turn behind the bar, so I used to sit in the members club and do my knitting. As you can imagine, I got to know some of the members really well and so it was brilliant to have my 21st birthday party there and celebrate with family, friends, and members of the golf club.

The first school I can remember going to was, a primary school in Cottingley and when I left there, I went to Redwood Croft special school near Wakefield until I was sixteen years old. My favourite lessons were music and drama. Once, we did a school play where I played Eliza Doolittle in," My fair lady" and I can still remember one of the songs that I sung in that play; "All I want is a room somewhere." I absolutely loved it!

Swimming was another of my favourite lessons and I loved that swimming pool which I thought was big, but everything looks big when you are a small child! As well as swimming, I loved playing netball and hockey and girls from other schools used to come to our school to play games against us. That was when I had lots of energy and I could run around the hockey and netball pitches, but I really don't think I could do that now.

When I was at Redwood Croft school, I met a boy called Nigel and we were very good friends for many years. We used to go to horse riding for the disabled together and one time I told Nigel that he reminded me of Rhett Butler from "Gone with the wind."

I used to stay at Nigel's house for the weekend with his mum and dad (Maureen and Kenneth) and every year we went on holidays abroad together and at the weekends we went out for meals. There was a local youth club called "New Horizons" which we both went to, right up to the time the funding ran out and it had to close. I loved spending time with Nigel but unfortunately after his parents died, he moved away to live with his sister, and we lost touch.

Chapter Two:
Moving into Adulthood

When I left Redwood Croft school, I went to the Park Lane College annexe where I enjoyed doing woodwork. It made me feel very proud to make my dad a coffee table which he absolutely loved. Drama was one of the other lessons that I did at college, and I am still part of a drama group today, called "Bright Sparks".

At Park Lane, I remember how I played the lead roles in two productions – "Christmas Past" and then "Phantom of the Opera" which was where I had to do a dance routine. Unfortunately, I didn't realise I had the costume on the wrong way round until someone pointed this out and I was so embarrassed when I had to go off stage to get changed. It wasn't funny at the time but I can laugh about this now.

The years I spent at this school was a happy time and when I heard that this school closed in 1991, it made me feel sad to think the school is not there anymore.

Up until the early 1980s, my parents ran a transport café in David Street, Holbeck, Leeds and my sister Jacqui worked there as well. This café was very well known around the Leeds area where they served up to 500 customers a day. Lots of people who worked for the Gas Board, Central Electricity Generating Board and BT, used to come here for breakfasts and lunch. Some workers from these local firms didn't have offices, so our café was a meeting place for them. It was a very, very, busy and well-known café and some of the local firms still keep in touch with my sister. Recently she told me that if you speak to anyone who has lived around Holbeck they will always say, "oh, I remember your café and your lovely family." We were and still are a very close family.

When I was 17, I came home from college one day and looked at my mum asleep on the settee. At least I thought she was asleep, but I couldn't wake her up, so I shouted to dad to ask if mum was okay. Dad rushed in and started crying and I stood there feeling cold. I couldn't speak and I didn't know what to do so I just went to my bedroom. I must have been in shock as I can't really remember much of what happened after that. My mum was only 60 years old when she died and this was the most awful time for me and all of our family.

My dad didn't think he could look after me on his own, so after the funeral, the decision was taken to sell the café and I went to live with my sister Jacqui and her husband Michael. Although I felt very sad and confused at this time, I loved being with my sister, and I still live with them both today.

After I left Park Lane College, I went to Moor End Adult Training Centre which was a day service for people with disabilities on a big industrial estate near Leeds. We did things there like putting advertising leaflets in envelopes for a Catalogue company which we got paid £2.70 a week for. Friday was the day when we all used to look forward to getting our pay packet, and at the time, I thought that was a lot of money for this work. We were all very upset when this work was stopped because the council thought the Catalogue Company were exploiting us. But we enjoyed it and felt we were doing something very useful.

Every morning I got picked up by a taxi to take me to the Moor End centre and I always sat in the front. One day the taxi driver took advantage of me and when it happened, I was shocked and confused and I just froze. When I got to Moor End, I broke down and started crying and I was taken into the office where they reported the incident and the police came to interview me. After I explained what had happened, they told me that if I went to court there wouldn't be enough evidence so they couldn't do anything. Those things that happened kept going round and round in my head and to this day I still get upset whenever I talk about it. It left me feeling like I didn't have a voice and this terrible experience had a really bad effect on me so after this happened my sister asked that I be transferred to West Ardsley Training Centre.

West Ardsley Training Centre gave me a second chance in life, and I really loved it there. The bad experience was always on my mind and because of what happened to me I think it was then that I decided I wanted to make a difference to the lives of people like me who don't have a voice when something bad happens to them. I really enjoyed my time at the West Ardsley Training Centre where we had a small café there serving tea, coffee, cakes and biscuits.

While I was at West Ardsley, I had the opportunity to study food and hygiene at Thomas Danby College (now called Leeds Thomas Danby) and I achieved City and Guilds certificates levels 1 and 2 in food safety. It was here that I first met Lucinda Yeadon who was the education and employment coordinator for Mencap Pathways. Lucinda Yeadon and a Mencap Pathways worker helped me to find work experience at the Morrisons Café in Leeds. I worked there for about two years, and to begin with, this was work experience but after a while I got paid. As I was only working a few hours each week, it didn't affect my benefits payments.

Morrisons café was always a very busy place and the thing I loved the most about working there, was serving customers their breakfasts from the hot counter. Later I worked as a waitress, clearing away the empty plates and cups and wiping down the tables. Unfortunately, I found standing up for too long very painful which is why I decided to stop working there even though it made me feel sad because I loved my job and made lots of friends. Even now, when my sister goes to Morrisons, people still ask about me and they talk about how I used to sit and do my knitting or embroidery during lunch breaks.

My next experience of work was at a local charity shop where I volunteered. To start with, I worked at the back of the shop sorting out clothes to put on hangers before they were passed onto another person who used a steamer to make them ready to go out on the shop floor. They were nice people there and I really enjoyed it but then I got a chance to work in an office doing some admin work. Although I felt proud to work in an office, I found this work experience hard because I struggled to follow their instructions. Unfortunately, I only worked there for a short time because I went on holiday and when I got back home, I was told that the firm had gone bust.

Chapter Three:
Self-Advocacy

After my time as an admin worker, I was told by Lucinda Yeadon that there was a fantastic job opportunity which they thought I might want to apply for. This job was working for CHANGE, a national campaigning charity for people with learning disabilities. The project was for two years, working full time and called "Making Partnership Boards Work."

Lucinda told me more about it and explained I would get paid a real wage and that she thought this job would be something I would enjoy. I really wanted to apply for this job, but I had already heard that a lot of people were applying but I applied anyway. I was over the moon when I was invited to go to Leeds for an interview.

I was full of confidence on the day of the interview and Lucinda came along with me. It was a really busy day and I was asked lots of questions which I can't remember now. I wasn't sure how well I'd done but I must have stormed it because I found out later that I'd got the job. I couldn't wait to get started.

CHANGE is a learning disability rights charity led by people with disabilities and the project I was employed to do was funded by Comic Relief for two years. Together with my co-worker we travelled around the country visiting self-advocacy groups and talking to them about their work with Partnership Boards.

Before I started working on this project, I didn't know much about self-advocacy. All I wanted was to make sure that people with a learning disability have the chance to speak out because society has always treated us differently and I wanted to change that.

Self-advocacy groups are a way for people with learning disabilities or autistic people, to speak out about things that are important to them both locally, nationally and internationally. They campaign for changes to local and national services, plan and deliver training and work with lots of different organisations to help make life better for everyone. These groups are often supported by local charities and are mostly led by people with learning disabilities and autistic people and linked to the Partnership Boards in their area.

This was a very special time for me. I loved travelling around the country with my co-worker, visiting self-advocacy groups in places like York, Oxford, Somerset and Cambridge. We talked to people about their experiences of Partnership Boards and helped them think about things they could do to make sure everyone was included. We told them about Easy Read and how they could do this to make sure information was easy to read and understand.

I learned a lot about the importance of self-advocacy groups and the work they were involved in with their Partnership Boards.

When the project finished, I felt very sad as I missed the work I was doing there, and it was a really difficult process to get my benefit payments set up again.

I first met Janet Wright and Louise Mills who worked for the joint commissioning service in Leeds when I was at CHANGE. When they heard that my job was coming to an end, they invited me to come and work for them one day a week to do filing and printing. It was around this time that I heard that Leeds Learning Disability Partnership Board was looking for a new co-chair.

Learning Disability Partnership boards are an opportunity for people with a learning disability, their families, carers and people who work with people with a learning disability to work together to improve the lives for everyone. Leeds City Council and NHS Leeds are the main funders of work commissioned by this Partnership Board.

I had to apply for this role, and then I was invited to an interview. They asked me lots of questions so it was another very busy but exciting day. When I was told I was going to be the co-chair of the Leeds Learning Disability Partnership Board you can imagine how happy I felt. Although I wasn't going to be paid, except for expenses, I knew it was something I really wanted to do because it was a way for me to make changes happen. What I really love, is listening to people and helping them find ways to get their voices heard so being a co-chair of the Partnership board was an important job and a brilliant opportunity for me.

During my time as co-chair of the Partnership Board I co-chaired meetings with independent co-chairs. This meant that the two people leading the meetings were someone with a learning disability and someone independent from the services represented at meetings. My first co-chair was George Wood followed by Derek Thomas, Lucinda Yeadon, Adam Ogilvie and then Councillor Khan.

Whenever there was a new independent co-chair, I introduced them to people and showed them how the Partnership Board worked. Adam Ogilvie reminded me recently that after introducing everyone at the beginning of meetings, we used to start with a warmup dance to get people moving as I knew that this would get people interested and feel ready to take part in the meeting.

The board meetings were always very busy and as a co-chair it was my job to make sure everyone had the chance to have their say and keep to the agenda. I also had to make sure that everyone understood the discussions and see if anyone had any questions. This is quite hard when lots of people want to speak at once or want to ask a question, so I had to keep looking round to see who had their hands up waiting to talk.

The Partnership Board always has a list of "key priorities" which are the main things they want to work on to improve lives for people with learning disabilities who live in Leeds. These "key priorities" when I was a co-chair, were around **Improving Health, Being safe, Having a life** and **Being Independent.**

The Reference group, later called, the Peoples Parliament, met four times a year and this was a chance for people with a learning disability and autistic people to come together with specially invited guests to talk about the "key priorities" the Leeds Partnership Board were working on.

Winterbourne View was a care home which was exposed in a BBC Panorama programme in 2012. It showed people with learning disabilities and autistic people being abused by staff. When I watched this programme I felt sick and really angry. It was heart breaking to see people being treated in this way and like a lot of people, it made me feel that society think that if you have a learning disability or autism then you do not matter.

After the report came out to find out what happened at Winterbourne View, a lot of work was done by learning disability partnership boards across the country to make sure that something like this didn't happen again. Unfortunately, we still hear about really bad things that happen to people with a learning disability or autistic people, so it's important to continue to work together to stop this happening.

I met some great people in my time at the partnership board, for example, Lucinda Yeadon, Janet Wright, Louise Mills, Maggie Graham, and Kath Lindley. Kath was the manager of Tenfold which is the learning disabilities forum in Leeds for voluntary sector organisations and she told me recently that she couldn't have done her job as well as she did without me. It was Kath who put me forward for the "Outstanding Contribution" award for Tenfold and she also put Leep1 up for other awards which I will tell you about later.

Our work in Leeds started with very few opportunities for people with learning disabilities but as you will see these opportunities grew very quickly and it's great to see organisations and people across Leeds, working together to make a difference.

Links for further information (scan QR codes)

CQC report on Winterbourne View confirms its owners failed to protect people from abuse - Care Quality Commission

CHANGE easy read document

Partnership Board - Through the Maze (through-the-maze.org.uk)

Learning Disability England – Stronger, Louder, Together!

Chapter Four:
Speaking Out!

The next amazing thing that happened was that Lucinda Yeadon started to talk about having a Great Council Chamber Take Over (this is now called the People's Parliament). She thought this would be an opportunity for council members to hear from people with autism and learning disabilities as the council members had very little experience of what our lives were like. The first chamber "Take Over" took place during Learning Disability week in 2010 and this was our chance to speak out and make changes happen.

I was the chair (in charge) of these meetings, and I think at the beginning members of Leeds City Council were a bit worried about allowing people with a learning disability to take over the council meetings. It was a big thing for them to do this, but it really did raise awareness of all the things we thought needed to change to make sure we had the same life chances as everyone else.

Over 50 adults with a learning disability and autistic people came to the Council Chamber Take Over. I really loved having politicians, like the MP Hilary Benn, at these meetings because I really felt they wanted to hear what we had to say. We all had lots of things that we were worried about, so we needed them to work with us to make things change for the better and we felt that the "Take Over" really did this.

Along with Kath Lindley and Maggie Graham, who was the Mencap campaigns manager, we talked to the politicians there and tried to get them to help us raise awareness of these important issues. If you saw me at the Council Chamber, you would see me looking round to see who wanted to speak next, shouting" Order, Order", when it got too noisy and then banging the gavel to get everyone's attention. I absolutely loved it! Tom Riordan, who is the Chief Executive of Leeds City Council, told me he thought all the work I was doing was fantastic.

In June 2011, the MP for Leeds Central, Hilary Benn, wrote to ask if a group of us from the Leeds Council Chamber Take Over group would like to visit the Houses of Parliament. He organised it for a group of 20 people but when we looked at how much it would cost for us to travel to London by train, we realised it was too expensive. So, we wrote back to Hilary Benn and asked if he could send a letter to the rail company which he did, and it was a lovely surprise when we were told we didn't have to pay for all the train tickets.

We all had a great time in London, but this was more than a day out for us as it turned into something much more. As well as having a tour of the House of Commons, we went on a tour of the House of Lords and then we listened to Prime Ministers questions. This was when David Cameron was Prime Minister. We had lunch with a group of the Leeds MPs, and later we met with each individual Member of Parliament for the different areas of Leeds and this is where lots of brilliant conversations started.

Lucinda Yeadon was now a councillor responsible for adult health and social care in Leeds and I was so excited when she invited me to shadow her for a day to see what she did. It was an interesting day as we went to lots of meetings together. We met with the Deputy Director of Adult Health and Social care and attended the Leeds Involving People annual general meeting. We also visited a day service for adults with a learning disability and met with the chair of the health and social care scrutiny board.

Spending the day with Councillor Yeadon, gave me so much confidence and it felt good that people with a lot of power were listening to me and other people who have a learning disability. So, not long after this I went to a meeting at SHINE, in Leeds, where the MP Ed Balls was speaking. Before I met Ed Balls, I wasn't sure what he would be like but when I heard him talk about social care, I realised that he was someone we needed to work with.

I'm the sort of person who never misses an opportunity to talk to someone, so at the end of the meeting, I went with Maggie and Kath to speak to Ed Balls. After a quick chat, I felt confident enough to ask him if I could shadow him for the day. Straight away Ed said, "yes, of course", and in July 2012, I finally got the opportunity to spend the day with him. He looked after me really well and treated me like a V.I.P. which made me feel wonderful. It was an amazing day as I went round with him to lots of different meetings in Morley and Outwood. He had an office in Morley, and at lunchtime we went out for sandwiches and then we sat down together to eat these in his office.

After I spent the day with Ed in his constituency, I was so excited when I received an invitation on official House of Commons notepaper to invite me to a barbecue at his house. When I arrived, there were already lots of people there and Ed was in his shorts and apron doing all the cooking. Ed made a real fuss of me and introduced me to his wife, Yvette Cooper, his friends, and local councillors and then after everyone had eaten, I sat and watched as the children and some of the adults' played games together.

The sun was shining all day long and I was so happy. It was a day I will never forget as I felt proud and honoured to be there amongst so many lovely people.

BBC - Takeover of Leeds council chamber

Scan me

https://youtu.be/UZtGpqm3oUY

Scan me

Chapter Five:
Leep1

Leeds advocacy (now called Advonet) is in a main office on an industrial site on Roundhay road in Leeds across from where café Leep is now. Between 2006 and 2010, lots of changes were happening for people with learning disabilities and their families. There was less money being spent on day services as personal budgets were introduced and people were given more choices about what they wanted to do each day. Councils across the country were looking at more meaningful ways for people with learning disabilities to spend their days.

Lots of day services began to close, and in 2010 the day service I went to in West Ardsley closed. We were given a choice to go to smaller sites across the area and I went to Leeds advocacy, with just two more people to talk about what we wanted to do. I worked closely with a gentleman called Paul who was CEO of Leeds Advocacy at the time. He became a director for Leep1, and he supported us for a few years at Leep1 before Leeds Advcocay became Advonet.

He helped us to set up the self-advocacy group, where people can get their voices heard. Everyone thought this was a great idea, so we talked about how we were going to do this. With help from Paul, we started writing letters and sent out emails to ask if anyone wanted to come along to our meetings and talk about things they wanted changing. Then we needed a name for our group, and after lots of discussions we all agreed to call our group **Leep1** which stands for Leeds People First.

Lee stands for Leeds, **P** stands for people and **1** means that we are people first.

As our group got bigger, we were given an office to work from where we could have our meetings and where people talked about things they wanted to do. The main thing people wanted to do was to find something fun which everyone could enjoy. We thought about having a games day where people could get together, meet up with their friends and have fun.

During this time, Amanda Haigh (Mandy) joined us first as a volunteer, then as a support worker before she went on to become a manager. Mandy was brilliant at getting us funding. It didn't take her long to find the money we needed so we could afford a bigger room where café Leep is now, to use as a games room. We ran a games day every Tuesday where we played games like badminton, table tennis, Bingo, draughts, and karaoke. We charged a small fee for people who came along and there was a small tuck shop where we sold sweets and drinks. Every week we went to Leeds to buy the sweets and drinks for the tuck shop, and I remember one time we had so much stuff in our bags that I nearly did the splits going down the escalator.

One of the members of Leep1 said they wanted more opportunities to have a job, so we talked about whether people would be interested in working in a café. We all thought this was a brilliant idea, so we went to a local café, looked at the menu and chatted to the people there to ask how they set it up and find out what we would have to do if we had the money to run a café. After talking to lots of different people, Mandy wrote a funding bid so that we could set up a café in the building where Leep1 met each week. It was a while before we heard back but we were so excited when we were told we had the money to start Café Leep.

Café Leep is now an accredited training employment training café which supports adults with learning disabilities and autistic people to train for their NVQs so they can go on to get paid employment in other cafes, restaurants, and pubs. In 2017, Café Leep won the best café award across the whole of Yorkshire and Humber. What an achievement!

At one of our meetings, members of Leep1 talked about where we wanted to go for a night out and we decided we wanted to go to a night club. Everyone has a right to go to clubbing if they want to but at the time there was only one nightclub, we could go to which was held just twice a year at Leeds University. We wanted a proper nightclub because the only other place we could go to dance and have fun was called a youth club and we were all adults. So, we visited the Tiger, Tiger, nightclub in Leeds, checked it was wheelchair accessible, spoke to the people there and then Mandy wrote a funding bid, this time to Leeds Community Foundation for £3000.

When we were awarded this money, we ran our first monthly nightclub in 2013 and on the first night over 200 people turned up. My job was to meet and greet people, tell them where the toilets were, mingle with people and sell tickets for the raffle. We were lucky to get some fantastic raffle prizes from Leeds Rhinos and Leeds United Football Club. Each month we chose a different theme for the nightclub where people dressed up in fancy dress to represent their favourite film character or pop star and everyone looked amazing. A band which was made up of people with a learning disability used to play at our nightclub evenings and they were incredible. We also held karaoke nights and on Valentine's Day we held a date night where people could try to find a partner.

It was such a shame when we heard that Tiger Tiger was closing down so we looked for other nightclubs in the city. We visited Pryzm who were really welcoming to us so we set up a nightclub there. During lockdown Pryzm changed ownership and eventually closed down, so we had to find a different nightclub called Pop World which was much smaller than the room we had in Pryzm but it was still accessible. This nightclub event still happens every month, with the same themed evenings and is just as popular as it was in the other nightclubs. We had some great volunteers who helped us and both Mandy and I absolutely loved these nights because everyone got so much from them.

Links to information

Advonet

The Advonet Group - Providing Independent Advocacy in Leeds

Leep1

Leep1 - Supporting adults with learning disabilities to speak up for themselves

Chapter Six:
Campaigns and Awards

I've been very lucky to meet some lovely people in my life and I first met Maggie Graham, when she was the Campaigns manager for Mencap. This is when I started to get more involved in local and national campaigns and one of the first events I went to where I gave a speech, was at Pudsey Town Hall. In 2003, the Criminal Justice Act made hate crime against people with a learning disability a law. The speech I gave was about hate crime and there were about 200 people in that hall. It was scary at first, but it felt so good to speak to so many people. Over the years I've become much more confident at speaking to a large audience, and I am always happy to answer questions but If I don't agree with what is being said I will say so. The main thing I want to get across is that people with a learning disability have a voice, we are entitled to speak out as much as anyone is.

In 2011, Mencap launched the "Stand by Me" campaign to stop hate crime against people with a learning disability and I took part in this campaign. We put together a list of ten promises for the police to sign up to which would show their commitment to end hate crime. These promises were for all police forces across the country to promise they would improve the way they dealt with hate crimes when people with a learning disability report them.

One of the women who came to Leep1 told us she was a victim of mate crime. Mate crime is when someone pretends to be your friend, but they do things to take advantage of you, like taking money from you or getting you to do things for them. This is treated as a hate crime by police. This woman said she had been drinking in a pub and a group of people pretended to be her friend. They got her to buy them drinks, then they went back to her house where they took all her money and bank cards. When another person told us they had been a victim of hate crime we decided to start a campaign to warn other people.

The first thing we did was to make a Rap. We all chose the words we wanted in the Rap and recorded this with an Indian drummer who was a drummer for the Stone Roses back in the day. He helped us to do the music along with his son who worked for BBC radio. Together we put the Rap to music, and we made and then showed this film at a hate crime conference. We wore these really big chains like rappers wear and I stood up and spoke about the brilliant work we had all done. Everyone loved our film, so we started showing it at other places too. We ran a hate crime session in Leeds market when we did quizzes to get people talking about hate crime. Then we were lucky to be able to use Metro buses to make a film about hate crime on a bus. We did a lot of takes as you can imagine, and it was a lot of fun but the message of the film was to show how hate crime can happen and what you can do if you are a victim of hate crime.

Once we made the film, we worked with a theatre group called "Bright Sparks" to develop this into a play which was funded by Safer Leeds. Then we went into primary schools to show this play because we wanted to work with these young people before they became teenagers. We wanted them to know how behaving in a certain way really affects someone's life for a very long time.

We took this film around quite a few schools, and we would do two performances – one was about hate crime and one was about mate crime. The first one was a bus scene and then we would stop the bus scene just as the person was about to be bullied and we asked the children "what do you think will happen here?" and "what should you do?" The children all came up with some fantastic answers which made it all worthwhile.

Because of this work, Leep1 were asked to take the lead on the Leeds Partnership Boards "being safe" strategy where we met with adult social care commissioners, members of the safeguarding board, and safeguarding leads from the hospital. People with learning disabilities co-chaired these meetings with Councillor Kevin Ritchie and together we started to make changes. Although things have got better, there is still a lot more work to do because hate crime hasn't gone away,

I went on rally's too which I think is a powerful way to get lots of people to listen and encourage them to do something that will make changes happen. In 2011, I joined the Hardest Hit rally in Leeds against government spending cuts affecting disabled people. The MP Hilary Benn for Leeds central was one of the key speakers where over 400 people took part. I was on the steps with Hilary Benn, and I gave a short speech. During lockdown, I interviewed Hilary Benn MP for my podcast I called Don't Dis my Ability and this is still available to watch on YouTube.

In 2014, I chaired the Mencap Hear my Voice campaign with the MP Ed Balls in Morley Town Hall. It was a powerful meeting and when it finished, he posted a video on YouTube. He said, "I'm not going to give a speech today because Susan is". Then he explained that he was going to campaign for better skills and jobs for people with learning disabilities and learn the lessons from the abuse at Winterbourne View. I was introduced as his friend and Ed spoke about how brilliant he thought my speeches were and how he loved watching me shout "Order, Order" in the Council Chambers to get everyone to shut up.

We launched the Being Me campaign in 2018 to get the message out there to show that we are all equal. Around this time, we launched a film called **Get Me** which was about what people liked doing and what their favourite things were. We did this to remind people that we are all human beings, and we all have a voice. With the right opportunities, everyone can speak out.

My life wasn't all campaigns and meetings though as another exciting thing happened when Maggie and I were invited as V.I.P. guests in 2013 to the opening night of the First Direct Arena in Leeds. Bruce Springsteen was the headline act, and he was brilliant. There were so many people there and the noise they made when he came on the stage is hard to describe as it was a noise I had never heard before. Everyone was so excited, they were singing along and dancing in the aisles, shouting and screaming and hugging each other. That's another night I will never forget.

I'm so proud of all the work I do to raise awareness of what people with a learning disability can do but it's lovely when I get nominated for awards.

In 2010 I was the runner up, for the Yorkshire woman of Achievement in the Jane Tomlinson category for Courage. I was nominated in recognition for the all the self-advocacy work I was involved in across Leeds. The awards ceremony was held in the Leeds Armoury, and it was a fabulous evening where I met many celebrities, and I had my photo taken with some of them. When my name was called out, I got a standing ovation and I felt so proud that I couldn't stop smiling.

In 2013 I was a finalist in the Leeds Legends award to highlight everything I've done to make a difference to the lives of people in my community. Even though I didn't win these awards I still felt that to get this far was a great achievement!

Café Leep won awards too. In 2017, they won the best café award out of 500 cafes across Yorkshire and Humber and in 2020 they were a finalist in the Recruitment, Industry and Disability and Initiative awards.

Links to information (scan QR codes)

About Us | Bright Sparks Theatre Arts Company

Hate and Mate Crime Rap Leep1 (youtube.com)

Podcasts - Leep1

About Hate Crime - Stop Hate UK

[QR code]

Learning Disability - Campaigning - Our Impact | Mencap

[QR code]

https://www.youtube.com/watch?v=ne4P8l0PljE

Mencap 'Hear my Voice' with Ed Balls

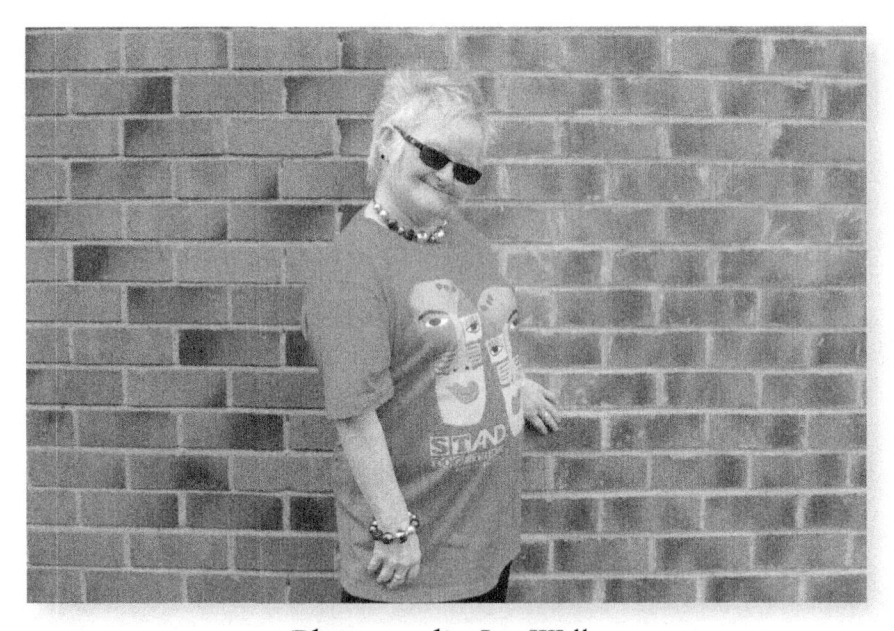

Photo credit: Jan Wells

Chapter Seven:
Training

I am passionate about making sure people with a learning disability are safe and I'm proud to be the Leeds safeguarding ambassador working alongside David Rickus from the Leeds Safeguarding Adults Board.

In 2020, the **Talk to Me, Hear My Voice** film was made by the Leeds safeguarding adult's board. This film is on YouTube and the cartoon image is based on me.

Sometimes people with a learning disability are not listened to or do not understand they are being abused. They often don't know what to do if they feel something is wrong. I want people to know they are being listened to and that information is explained to them in a way they understand to keep them safe. Because of what happened to me in the past I don't want this to happen to other people. When we do safeguarding training we give a presentation before we show the film and then we ask if they have any questions for us. I really enjoy this part of the training and love answering any questions directed at me.

In 2019, Leeds Safeguarding Adults Board won an award from Leeds City Council for excellence.

Being a self-advocate and co-chair of the Leeds Learning Disability Partnership Board made me want to get involved in politics and fight for the rights of people like me, so when I heard about the Tomorrows Leaders course, I wanted to apply for a place on it.

Tomorrow's leaders is a leadership course, run by Inclusion North, for people with a learning disability or autism who are already in a leadership role in their community. Being a leader is about being confident and passionate, find ways to make changes happen and share your skills with other people.

The course was written by a group of people from the National Forum in the early 2000's and they wanted to make sure that Tomorrows Leaders could be run by an organisation that could run it successfully. Inclusion North was gifted Tomorrow's leaders in about 2007 and I joined the course in 2010.

I applied to go on the course, and I was really happy when I was told I had a place on the next course which was in Durham. I went with Louise Mills, who I knew from the Partnership Board, and the course was held for a few days at a time every few weeks, so each time we went we had to stay overnight in Durham.

As part of the course, we were all asked to research an area in our community. I researched Meanwood Park hospital which was a long stay hospital for people with learning disabilities. My research project was called "Forgotten Lives." It was very depressing to read about this hospital because people who were there weren't given a choice to do things they wanted and there were very few opportunities like there are now. This made me feel very angry and upset but although it's closed now, I'm sure that people who were there won't forget about it.

I graduated at the end of the Tomorrows Leaders course and in 2013 and 2017 I was asked to come back to co-deliver the course with the Project Manager at Inclusion North. When I heard how much confidence this course had given people who had taken part and how much they had learnt, I felt so proud, and it was a real honour to share my experiences with others.

During the Covid19 pandemic, together with my friends at Café Leep, we trained over 70 police officers online in a short training session with Paul, our support worker. We told the police how some people with a learning disability will often be too frightened to speak to them and how important it is to talk clearly and slowly without using big words or jargon. After the training session, we got some amazing feedback from the police saying how much they enjoyed it and we really felt we'd made a difference.

In our group at Leep1 we talked about how we thought that letters from the NHS should be available in easy read because often people miss appointments as the letters are too difficult to read and understand. So, we worked with our local NHS trust to make their letters in easy read, and we worked on a short piece of drama to show staff how to talk to people with a learning disability. Our support worker, Paul practiced this drama with us before we went out and our main message was to say that if we are a patient, it's not right to talk to our support worker or family member instead of us. We got some good feedback from this drama, and we really enjoyed doing it.

A few years ago, I felt down, depressed, teary, forgetful, and scared. I didn't know what was happening to me but when I told someone how bad I was feeling, they told me about the menopause. One of our support workers at café Leep explained that symptoms of the menopause aren't often picked up if you have a learning disability or autism. So, we set up a woman's health group to offer support to women there going through the menopause to learn more about what we can do to help ourselves.

We talked about diets, feeling sad, the different treatments people said helped them and when we promoted it on social media lots of people were very interested to hear what we were doing. It was exciting when we were invited to go on BBC Breakfast to be interviewed. The interview took place at café Leep and I talked about the menopause, how I was feeling and how important it is to raise awareness of it. This was not just to raise awareness for other people like me but also for people like parents, carers, nurses, and doctors.

In 2017 I was asked to do the voice over for the NHS 111 film to help autistic people and people with a learning disability learn more about how to use this service. I was really excited to do this, and I think this is a really good film with great acting from local people.

Links to information (scan QR codes)

[QR code]

Inclusion North - inclusion for people with a learning disability or autism

[QR code]

Supporting people to be safe from abuse and neglect in Leeds. - YouTube

[QR code]

BBC Breakfast - Down's Syndrome Association Menopause feature - YouTube

[QR code]

NHS 111 An Inclusive Service - YouTube

Photo credit: Jan Wells

Chapter Eight:
Fashion Design

I love buying and trying on clothes. When I go shopping, I like to see the latest fashions and think about how I can make them myself. Making and designing clothes is something I really enjoy doing because it makes me feel calm whenever I feel stressed.

I started the creative hands group at Leep1 when I began to bring in my sewing, knitting and embroidery to show the group and some people there were interested in what I was doing. So, I got the idea to start a workshop to show anyone who wanted to, how to sew and knit which is how the creative hands group started. We met on a Wednesday morning, and someone brought their own work in and as we chatted together someone else said they wanted to learn cross stitch. I taught her how to thread a needle and do cross stitch and then as a group we worked together to embroider a tablecloth.

As we had a good connection with our local hospital, we thought it would be a great idea to upcycle nurses' uniforms. We were invited to the hospital in Leeds and the nurses there gave us their old uniforms which we took back to the group. It was exciting to think about what we could make with these uniforms, and together we made lots of different outfits. In Learning Disability week, we put on a fashion show at our monthly nightclub which was a great success, and everyone was so impressed with all the different outfits we made.

During lockdown, Mandy wrote a bid for funding from the postcode lottery, as a group of us at Leep1 wanted to make clothes we could sell on the internet which would have a positive message about disability. We wanted to set up a clothing brand that would have a positive message about disability and what we can achieve so we chose the name A.N.D. which stands for **A**bility **N**ot **D**isability. We worked with Amanda Burton who led this project, and she won The Creative Award for her work with us over lockdown.

There are eight of us in the AND group and we were involved right from the start of this process. We drew pictures of the images we wanted to appear on the T-shirts, hoodies, bags and sweatshirts and then these were uploaded digitally to appear on the clothing and bags.

We sell our clothing on eBay and Kirkgate market in Leeds. Selling our clothing and bags to customers gave me lots of confidence and when I make a sale it makes me feel so proud. One of the top selling designs was one I made with the words across the front in big letters saying – **You will turn out ordinary if you are not careful**.

If you want to find out more about AND clothing, you can visit their website and read their book "AND" which is available on Amazon.

AND Clothes - Leep1

Scan me

Photo credit: Jan Wells

Chapter Nine:
My Next Steps

The last few years have been amazing and although I made the choice to leave Leep1 last year, I am still very busy. This was an extremely sad time for me as three of the staff I had worked alongside with for many years left and one of these was Mandy.

Thankfully, I was asked to become a director for Inspired-Nation CIC which is a social enterprise that Mandy set up after she left Leep1 together with Jan Wells. This meant I was able to still see Mandy and be involved in her new projects. We went to Roundhay Park to do our first photo shoot for their new website and Jan Wells took some fantastic photos of me and my sister.

I had always wanted to write my own story about my journey of campaigning and how I became an ambassador for learning disabilities in Leeds. I spoke about it many years ago to Mandy and Karen Murray. This was when Karen came along to Leep1 to deliver some of her advocacy games when we had our game's day. She worked with a self-advocacy organisation in Harrogate and brought some of her games that got our members talking and speaking up about the way they would behave in certain situations. She had written her own book called 'When Amy Met Gary" and the book is about four characters with learning disabilities and the struggles they face in their everyday lives. It's a fantastic book for people to understand the difficulties we often face, and this got me wanting to write my own book which I talked to Karen about.

At the time, Karen was very busy, but she got back in touch with Mandy recently as she had seen some of the work she was doing on LinkedIn, and they met online. Karen has moved out of the area now and has retired but agreed to help me finally write my story. We've worked together with weekly video calls to help me tell my story and spoke to other people who have been important in my life to help me fill in some of the gaps. Both Mandy and I cannot thank her enough for all the work she has put in to create my dream of becoming an author. Funny how these things happen when it was just a thought all those years ago.

Inspired-Nation ran their first project at Living Potential Farm which was a mindfulness retreat, and I attended. I felt like I needed some self-care and time to relax, and the retreat helped me to do just that. The retreat was in woods with a wooden wellness cabin and was such a beautiful location. I spent the day with friends and learnt lots of different tools to help me relax and take care of myself. We did meditations, laughter yoga, confidence on camera, and talked about the benefits of being in nature.

The next project I became involved in was Alpac-able. My sister, Mandy and Jan went along to a farm which belonged to my sister's best friend to take some photos of me and their alpacas. This was for a new project creating digital art called NFT's which stands for Non-Fungible Tokens. They are sold online instead of in a physical gallery, and we named the digital art Alpac-able because I wanted to promote our abilities through the artwork this was why we added 'able' on the end. We had a lovely day shooting pictures at the farm and got some great shots. There was one that got hundreds of likes on Facebook which was me holding one of the alpacas. After the shoot we chose the best picture of an alpaca which I decided to draw. It was then made into an alpaca NFT, and we named it "Alpac-able".

Photo Credits: Jan Wells

During this time, we were all introduced to a young entrepreneur who was into web3 and NFT's who became interested in what we were doing and wanted to support our project. Inspired-Nation wanted to support 16 more adults with learning disabilities to create NFT's which is essentially digital art which is sold online. They wrote a funding bid to The Arts Council and were successful.

I am now creating digital art which was displayed and showcased at Left Bank Leeds in November 2023, and I was thrilled to be finally recognised as an artist. We worked with an art teacher called Kerri Butterworth who I had worked with before and she always makes her sessions so much fun. The group all explored different types of art so that we could choose which technique to use for our final pieces. We have partnered with Leeds 2023 as it is the year of culture in Leeds, and it will mean more people will hear about our exhibition and hopefully attend. It's so exciting!

I still work closely with Advonet and their "Asking You" service. This is an opportunity for people with a learning disability to help make services better for everyone. This is something I am passionate about because services need to hear from people like me who can tell it like it really is.

One other thing I really love doing is drama and I'm proud to be a member of Bright Sparks theatre group. The latest show I am rehearsing for is "Sheets Across the Streets" and is about the history of communities in Leeds and how they lived their lives.

I love my life and I love what I do. There are still so many exciting things I am ready to get involved with and I can't wait to get started!

www.inspired-nation.co.uk

Asking You! - Part of The Advonet Group

Sheets Across The Streets | Bright Sparks Theatre Arts Company

Photo Credit: Jan Wells

Chapter Ten:
My Brilliant Sister!

Jacqui Ward writes;

When Susan was born, I was only 16 years old and did not quite understand the implications of a baby with Downs Syndrome. As I was the oldest of 4 children my Mum tried to explain to me that Susan would have very limited learning capacity and would only have a very short lifespan. Well Susan certainly has defied all that!

Unfortunately, our mum passed away very suddenly when Susan was only 17 years old. It came as a big shock to all the family as we knew there was going to have to be some life changing decisions. Personally, I had to make a very big decision as our dad was unable to cope with Susan, so after a discussion with my husband, it was decided that Susan would come to live with us at our home.

Susan has brought so much joy to both of us as unfortunately we were unable to have children of our own. It's funny how God works in mysterious ways.

Susan brings joy to everyone she meets and tries to do her very best despite her disability. She puts 110% into everything she does, she makes us so proud of her achievements. One memory in particular will stay with me forever was when Susan was nominated for the Yorkshire Woman of Achievement - The Jane Tomlinson award for Courage. When they called out her name she walked down to the stage, and the choir were singing Climb Every Mountain. There was not a dry eye on our table, and I still get very emotional when I think about it.

Susan has achieved so much in her lifetime, overcoming quite a lot of obstacles along the way, including harassment, prejudices, and bullying, but she is determined to get the voices of people with a learning disability heard and still to this day Is the Advocate for people with Learning Disabilities for Leeds City Council.

Susan has lived with me and my husband now for 41 years and to say that I am extremely proud of her is an absolute understatement, as she never stops giving. Some people say to me Susan Is lucky to have you, my reply to them is **No.** I am the lucky one for having her in my life!

Photo Credit: Jan Wells

Chapter Eleven:
A Truly Inspiring Person

Maggie Graham writes;

I first got to know Susan when I began working for Mencap in 2003. I think the first time we met was at a Partnership Board meeting. I worked in the community development team at Mencap, and later in the campaigns team. Susan and I worked together on many different things. She was a fantastic spokesperson for the national Mencap campaigns I was involved with about health, employment, disability hate crime and cuts in social care. She was involved with lots of events and was interviewed on the radio.

We worked with many people in and around Leeds, often with Kath Lindley from Tenfold. We always had a lot of fun as well as doing the 'serious' stuff. One of the best things was being invited to go with Susan and friends to the Yorkshire Women of Achievement Awards. It was a fantastic moment watching her collect an award for her work as an ambassador for people with a learning disability.

Council Chamber Takeovers - as the chair of the Partnership Board, Susan was the obvious choice to co-chair several of these events with the Lord Mayor, I think the first one was in 2010? Lucinda Yeadon, who was a councillor, helped to make it possible. It was a really big thing to take over the Council Chamber, it had never been done before and it had such a big impact. It gave people with a learning disability the chance to experience being a councillor and a platform to talk about the issues that mattered most to them.

About a dozen people with a learning disability spoke on a range of issues to about 100 people with a learning disability, and the meeting was run much like a full council meeting. People sat in the councillors' seats and voted on the issues that meant so much to them. Afterwards, we took a delegation to a real full council meeting, to tell the councillors what people had said. Susan chaired the events and led the delegation with such confidence, she really inspired the councillors to do something positive about people with a learning disability.

During this time, Kath, Susan and I went to an event in York to hear **Jon Bercow**, the then Speaker of the House of Commons. Afterwards, Susan asked him if he'd like to chair a council chamber takeover with her! He was delighted to be asked and said yes! We finally welcomed him in July 2013, and opened up the 'takeover' to people from the north of England, it was a really big event. Jon and Susan were a great double act, I remember she was very good at keeping him in his place! He was so impressed by Susan's skills and the overall day had a big effect on him.

Meeting Leeds MPs - Hilary Benn MP sponsored a large group of us, including Susan, to visit the Leeds MPs at the House of Commons in 2011. We had a fantastic day. Over the following year, we had more meetings with the MPs in Leeds, to talk about the different campaigns we were involved with. Susan hit it off immediately with her MP, Ed Balls! Later that year, Susan went on to be a keynote speaker with Hilary Benn MP at the Hardest Hit protest in Leeds, about social care cuts. Standing on the steps outside of Leeds Town Hall, Susan spoke with her usual confidence to over 500 people who had come to the protest.

Ed Balls - Susan kept in touch with Ed Balls and when he heard she would like to be an MP, he invited her to come and spend the day shadowing him in the Morley and Outwood Constituency. Susan received the full VIP treatment, travelling with Ed to important meetings with many different groups throughout the day. I waited for her at the Labour Meeting in Morley that evening. She looked fresh as a daisy and every bit the MP in her red suit. When it was Ed's turn to speak to the meeting, he stepped aside and asked Susan to do it for him! Susan did not hesitate to accept and was brilliant, of course.

I was very touched when Susan invited me to a special evening in 2013. She had been given two free tickets to the opening night of the Leeds First Direct Arena. It was a concert by **Bruce Springsteen** and we had a lovely evening. We'd never been in such an enormous place; it was quite overwhelming to be in such a massive crowd.

When I went to work for NHS England, Susan very kindly agreed to do the 'voice-over' for a film about how to use the NHS

111 service. The film was specially made for people with a learning disability and autistic people. Susan did an amazing job with the voice-over. That film has now been watched by over 45,000 people!

I am so lucky to have worked with and become friends with Susan. She is a truly inspiring person.

Photo Credit: Jan Wells

Chapter Twelve:
Susan Hanley is a Legend!

K ath Lindley writes;
I first met Susan when I started working for the then called Leeds voluntary Sector Learning Disability Forum, (we later changed our name to the much more accessible Tenfold!) I think the first time I ever met her was at an event in Pudsey Town Hall, and she absolutely blew me away with her passion, her big personality and wicked sense of humour and her total honesty about what it is really like to be a woman with a learning disability – she doesn't hold back! The other thing that struck me about her was her impeccable dress sense – she is always so well-groomed and well turned out, and she continues to this day!

For many years Susan was the CEO / Co-Chair of Leep1, and so I had the great pleasure of working with her on many different campaigns and initiatives to improve the lives of people with a learning disability, working closely with a wide range of

VCSE organisations in the city. She was, and probably still is, the best-known face of learning disability, and always speaks out with conviction and passion. She is a true ambassador and a great advocate for other learning-disabled people.

One of the key things I worked with Susan on were the Council Chamber Take Over Days – which were just amazing! Susan chaired these massive events on many occasions. She would sit in the mayor's chair and use the gavel to respectfully ask for people for 'Order!' Susan could always be relied on to handle people with decorum and to keep the event running on time, and we worked together to develop her script for the day, which she read out clearly and confidently. Susan has a keen interest in politics and led a group of learning-disabled people on a visit to attend the Houses of Parliament, even going to Prime Ministers Question Time! She shadowed the then Shadow Chancellor of the Exchequer, Ed Balls for the day, and he told me that he had learned far more from her than she would ever do from him! She went on to be a guest at Ed and Yvette's Garden party, something I know she is immensely proud of.

Susan loved going to the annual Yorkshire Women of Achievement Awards and I nominated her for an Award one year. She didn't win, (although she SHOULD have!), but received a Highly Commended prize – the first woman with a learning disability to ever do so. At these types of events, Susan loved to 'hob nob' with TV royalty, meeting the cast of Emmerdale and Calendar on several occasions – but she was always far more of a celebrity than any of them ever were!

Susan co-chaired the LD Partnership Board for many years; she led on many of the events that we developed to be part of learning disability week and was an award winner of the Outstanding Contribution Award at the Tenfold LD Awards in its inaugural year. She helped and supported me with many Campaigns, including 'Get Me' – Get a Better understanding of Learning Disabilities', which was a huge success. She was part of and spearheaded many health initiatives to improve health outcomes for learning disabled people and even appeared in several films to promote and encourage social change.

She is an inspirational and empowered woman; she is amazing; she is brilliant and funny and kind. And whilst small in stature, her impact has been HUGE!

I am truly honoured to know Susan and to have her as my friend. I miss her now that I work in Wakefield. She is unique, a fabulous role model and a real 'one off', and she has made such a massive difference to improving the lives of other people with a learning disability.

Chapter Thirteen:
A Brilliant Leader and Friend

Mandy Haigh writes;
I first met Susan when I became a volunteer at Leep1 in 2010 and this was my first introduction to the learning-disabled community. We sat down together, and I remember talking to her about her love for needlework and how my mum was a seamstress. We instantly hit it off as we had lots in common and I was excited to find out more about this interesting lady.

At the time Leep1 was managed by a lady named Bev who was on a secondment by Leeds City Council to manage the self-advocacy group. I wasn't sure what the purpose of the group was and at the time and there were only 5 people with learning disabilities that attended three days a week, Wednesday to Friday.

I began working there regularly two days a week and eventually Bev's contract ended, and her role came up as manager which I applied for and was lucky to be appointed.

I was so excited as I loved working with Susan and all the members of Leep1, they were such an inspiring bunch of people. The biggest thing I loved when working alongside people with learning disabilities was the fact that they take everyone at face value and are completely open, honest, funny and talented. People often think that because they have learning disabilities that they can't do many things, well this was not the case for the members of Leep1, in fact completely the opposite as I soon found out.

I began working alongside Susan to build Leep1 into a reputable organisation and it grew from delivering 3 days to 5. With Susan at the helm of everything she continued to inspire me with her grit and determination to show others that everyone can achieve in their life.

I supported her through a programme called Tomorrows Leaders where she showed others how to become leaders in their life. Of course, Susan was a wonderful advocate to show others how to speak up for their rights and tell people what they wanted from their lives. This is so important as not many people with learning disabilities have the confidence to do this.

Susan was the voice of Leep1 and campaigned for many changes during this time, one of these being the really important issue of menopause, Susan was interviewed by BBC Breakfast on how menopause can show up early in learning-disabled adults to raise awareness for carers and support staff to look out for the signs. She became an Ambassador within Leeds for people with learning disabilities and a well-known face within the city. I felt proud and privileged to have forged such a special relationship with such an inspirational woman.

Susan co-chaired many meetings with some important people and confidently spoke in front of a full Civic Hall in the council chambers. I admired her for her fearlessness.

One time we had the honour of presenting a deputation to the council on how Leeds City Council should lead by example and begin employing learning-disabled adults. There were three speakers with learning disabilities that day and they all did an incredible job, I was so proud of them all. At the end they received a standing ovation and a promise from Leeds City Councils mayor to make changes and support more employment opportunities for adults with learning disabilities within the city.

After lockdown, Susan started a podcast to connect with other self-advocacy groups across the UK. Hilary Benn and a learning disability nurse at St James hospital were interviewed on her podcasts talking about covid and how hard it had been for everyone.

One of the members of Leep1 became a victim of mate crime. Mate crime is hard to spot as they pretend to be your friend for their own personal gain, and it is done so slyly. It's such a terrible and devious crime and learning-disabled adults can be so vulnerable in these kinds of situations because they are so open to friendship.

After we were all told about how she had become a victim, Leep1 wanted to raise awareness of these crimes and took a touring show around year 11 primary school children. It was so powerful and got the children to understand the impact and trauma it can cause someone with a learning disability. I remember 1 young boy who came up to me after the show to tell me about some of the names the children called him. He was multi-cultural and the children called him dirty and told him to go get a wash. He didn't know this was wrong and a hate crime until we came along. Susan played the part of a bully on a bus tormenting and abusing another actor who played the victim, she played a great part in the show.

I left Leep1 in 2022 to pursue my own career and thankfully Susan agreed to become a director of my business, Inspired-Nation CIC. We are still close to this day and she has stayed a big part of our organisation and my life. Susan recently finished an art project and presented her artwork at an exhibition at Leftbank Leeds alongside 16 other artists. The event was an incredible evening and I felt so proud of all the artists who presented their artwork there.

Photo Credit: Jan Wells

Deputation to Leeds City Council to employ more learning-disabled adults within the city.

Council - Wednesday 15 January 2020, 1:00pm - Start video at 0:02:59 - Leeds City Council Webcasting (public-i.tv)

Innovate & Create - NFT art exhibition by learning-disabled and autistic adults (youtube.com)

Chapter Fourteen:
Telling Susan's story

Karen Murray writes;
I first met Susan in about 2010 when I attended workshops in York run by Inclusion North. At that time, I was working with self-advocacy groups in Harrogate and Craven and some people I was with recognised Susan. Over the years I often saw Susan at conferences, workshops and meetings at various venues including Leeds, York, Manchester and Birmingham and I couldn't fail to be impressed by how confident she was at speaking in front of large audiences and how people immediately warmed to her.

Through my conversations on social media with Café Leep, I was invited to their games day to share my self-advocacy games. It was here that I first met Mandy and Susan and she shared her desire for someone to help her write her life story. Unfortunately, as I was busy with other work, I was unable to help but I continued to visit Café Leep on several occasions and I loved observing

Susan with her bubbly personality and sense of fun as she moved amongst her friends and colleagues.

After I retired and moved away from North Yorkshire, I reconnected with Mandy who had by then left Café Leep and she asked me if I would be interested in helping Susan tell her life story. I agreed straight away, and we started to plan how we could do this by organising weekly internet calls with Susan and with other people who knew her well to start to piece together stories from her past.

Our weekly zoom calls were a time for Susan to recall some of her favourite memories and as I started to research Susan's life, I was amazed and inspired by just how much she has achieved. There were definitely some "wow" moments for me as she recalled her life experiences. Susan had forgotten some things that happened (as we all do) until we talked about information I'd found on internet searches or from the people we interviewed, and then all her memories came flooding back.

It has been an absolute pleasure to work with Susan, her family and friends to help her tell her story and I believe that between us we have given a real flavour of the amazing life experiences Susan has had and the people in her life who have been there to champion her. I know that although this is the end of her book, Susan has even more exciting projects that she is working on so … watch this space!

I have been so inspired by hearing about all of Susan's work whilst helping her to write this book. It has been an absolute honour to help her tell her story by capturing the moments from her life that mean so much to her.

Chapter Fifteen

Jan Wells writes:

Susan is an inspirational character. I first met her about 11 years ago and at that time she told me that she wanted to have a book written about her life, so I am very pleased for her that this has now happened.

Her story needed to be captured and over the years I have worked with her on different video projects, notably the Hate and Mate crime video which has been very seen widely since. Also, the AND project, I did quite a few photoshoots with Susan and the group. Most recently she was involved with the Inspired-Nation project Innovate and Create. Susan is very creative and did some brilliant designs for this project. I wish her all the best with her book, she definitely deserves the accolade!

Photo Credit: Jan Wells

Printed in Great Britain
by Amazon